DUNCAN STEWART

Your Hidden Mind

Discover Strategies to Enhance Your Well-being

This book was professionally typeset on Reedsy.
Find out more at reedsy.com

Contents

Introduction

Your Hidden Mind

Introduction.

This book is intended to give you the tools, techniques and strategies to set you on a journey of discovery to a more serene and fulfilling life. In today's parlance we might describe this as being in a state of well-being.

What does well-being mean? The Oxford English Dictionary defines it simply as:

well-being [noun] – the state of being comfortable, healthy or happy.

I believe that it can mean much more than this wholesome but simplistic definition.

On this journey we will delve into the mysteries of one of life's most powerful forces and explore the possibilities that are available to us all. Some would say that at one end of the spectrum anything is possible if these powers are unleashed. Others might say that health, wealth and happiness await us all if we can tap into this force and allow it to help us. We all have this force within us. I want to show you how to access it.

So, what is this life force? Drum Roll Please - our Subconscious Mind.

We all have one but most people are completely unaware of its function and potential to help us achieve the state of well-being. It works in cooperation and partnership with the conscious mind to, literally, keep us alive and function as a member of the Human Race.

Let me give you a very brief background to myself and the experience that led me to want to explore, and benefit from the power of the Subconscious mind.

I'm 73 years old and have been around the block several times. I have lived and worked in many parts of the world, all in the field of Facilities Management. I was heavily involved in the professionalization of the Facilities Management industry in the UK back in the mid 1980s and was a founder member of the professional representative body. I studied Industrial Psychology and Sociology at college together with Arboriculture and Land Management. I now act as a Consultant advising businesses to improve the way they manage their Facilities by adopting the methodology enshrined in the International Standards Organization (ISO) 41001 standard.

The experience I referred to above occurred when I was at school at about age 14. I traveled daily to and from school on the School Bus. I had the pleasure of traveling on the same bus with Mary, she was a Senior and two years older than me. She was kind, gentle, attractive and the school darling and everybody loved her. She left school and went on to University and married Hugh, her school boyfriend. From the day she left school I never saw Mary or Hugh, thought about them, or talked about them. Well not in any depth, why would I?

About 12 years later, on a Friday night, out of the blue, I dreamt about Mary. How strange! My wife was bemused (and maybe a bit jealous) and I was confused. Why on earth had I dreamt about her?

Hey, it's the weekend, things to do. So, off I pop to our nearest town to buy some stuff and yes - you have guessed correctly - I bumped into Mary & Hugh walking down the Main Street. They had traveled from their home in France and were here visiting parents. It was a delightful encounter, we had a coffee and a catch up and went our separate ways. I, for one, with a sense of contentment, mystery and intrigue and a thirst to understand. I remembered my college days and my first encounter with the mind. Where did I put those psychology textbooks?

Now, some people will say that was just a coincidence. However, since that encounter I have taken a view that the subconscious mind has abilities that we are not in control of, or even aware of; is the subconscious mind able to communicate with others?

Almost unbelievably I had a second episode just a few months ago. I was cutting the grass and out of nowhere a name just popped into my head. Graham M was a contemporary of mine during High School. Living in Florida he was not a great friend but we were team-mates for the Rugby 1st XV. As with Mary & Hugh I never thought about Graham since leaving school some 55 years ago. I spent a moment reflecting and then got on with cutting the grass. Imagine my shock, surprise and maybe even a touch of terror when a couple of days later up popped an invite to connect with Graham on Facebook. We are now back in contact albeit limited as I am not a fan of social media. Coincidence or what?

To this day, I have not understood what, seemingly, primordial force was at play that stretched across the globe. Just writing that sentence sends a shiver down my spine! Have you ever experienced anything like that? I may not have understood what was in play here but I am happy to concede that the subconscious mind may have powers way beyond my understanding.

Either way, I have used the subconscious mind and the methods I will describe to achieve a state of well-being that aligns with hopes, dreams and ambitions. No doubt you may be able to recount similar incidents, or maybe a sense of deja vu. One thing is certain, whatever goes on in your head between the conscious and subconscious minds is a powerful force.

One final point to make before we take the first step of our journey. How can we measure progress? The Scottish scientist and engineer Lord Kelvin (he of the Kelvin temperature scale, and no, I have no idea how that works) once said that "if you cannot measure you cannot improve" or words to that effect. I believe that one measure that I have used in other aspects of life may hold a clue. The phrase "The Quality of Life" is often banded about as being a key indicator on how good or bad life is. Clearly, this will be different for everybody. For some it will be the big house, fast car, trophy partner. For others it might be as simple as access to clean water. For me it is something completely different. It is the length of time between calamities, disasters, trouble, upsets etc. The longer the time gap between issues the better the quality of life!

For some it may still only be minutes or hours; for others it might be days, weeks or even months. I am confident that if you undertake this journey you will see the time gap in your quality life indicator increase.

So, strap in and enjoy the ride!

1

Chapter 1: Understanding the Subconscious Mind

This chapter could be a whole book in its own right but the point is to give just a brief insight into the powerhouse that is the subconscious mind. I look on the subconscious mind as the keeper of the secrets of existence. It houses deeply ingrained memories both good and bad, beliefs, and experiences that influence how we think, feel, and act. These subconscious patterns are often founded in childhood, shaping how we perceive ourselves and the world around us.

As an example, if you repeatedly heard, as I did, as a child that you were not clever enough to succeed, this belief may have become ingrained in your subconscious, influencing your sense of self-worth and approach to challenges. I was told this pretty much every day by my father. At my age I still marvel at what I have achieved despite his negativity. Thanks mainly to a supportive partner and an understanding of why I still feel this way on occasions.

Unlike the conscious mind, the subconscious doesn't analyze or question; it simply stores and retrieves information. It is shaped by experiences, memories, and the beliefs we've adopted over time

- whether we're aware of them or not.

Have you ever arrived at your destination having been on a regular journey by train or car, only to realize you don't remember the journey? That's your subconscious at work. It handles routine tasks, like breathing, circulation, digestion etc, freeing up your conscious mind for more complex decision-making. However, its influence goes far beyond routine actions. The subconscious mind is the source of automatic thoughts, emotional reactions, and habitual behaviors. These factors can either support or sabotage your well-being.

Appreciating the immense power of the subconscious mind is step one in realizing you have access to a force of unimaginable strength for personal growth and well-being. We have just scratched the surface here.

2

Chapter 2: Access to the Subconscious Mind

O K, so maybe now you feel as if you are sitting on a volcano, and maybe you are, because the journey begins now. This chapter is about tapping into this power house of your subconscious mind. Please do not be intimidated by, or dismissive of, these tried and trusted techniques.

1. Meditation

Meditation is one of the most effective ways to access the subconscious. When you meditate, you quiet the chatter of the conscious mind and create space to observe subconscious thoughts and feelings. To be clear, we are not dressed in red robes, sitting cross legged with our forefinger and thumb together going Hommmmmmmm! We do, however, need to sit or lie quietly in a comfortable space and still the body. Turn the phone off together with any other distractions and dim the lights or draw the blinds. Close your eyes and relax into the chair. Slow your breathing down and allow your body and mind to slow down and defog.

There are enough books to fill a library on the science and the "how to" of meditation and how it works. When I was first introduced to the practice I was very skeptical. I soon discovered that it can be very rewarding and effective. I now practice every day, even if it's just for five minutes; it calms my jumbled mind and brings about a state of serenity that sets me up for the day. I would urge you to try this and I guarantee that it will not hurt you or cost you - other than time, and that you will, like me, come to enjoy the experience.

Here are some quick tips for a successful meditation session:

- Create a supportive environment - even if it's just a dining chair in the kitchen/diner. Remember - phone off!
- Begin each session with a clear intention, such as "I want to release stress" or "I want to explore my inner beliefs." Or I just want to clear my mind".
- Slow, deep breaths help calm your nervous system and center your attention.
- Observe but don't judge thoughts or emotions that emerge. Instead of engaging with them, let them pass like leaves floating down a stream.
- Consistency is key. Even 10–15 minutes a day can create profound shifts over time.

I have found the benefits of meditation to be considerable and varied

- Reduces stress and anxiety by helping to put things in perspective
- Enhances self-awareness and encourages a sense of responsibility
- Improves focus and emotional regulation by helping to see both sides of the story.

Lastly, in this section, a master in the art of meditation once said that we should meditate for at least 10 minutes a day. He added that those people who claim they don't have the 10 minutes to meditate ***need*** to meditate for at least 20 minutes a day!

2. Affirmations and Positive Self-Talk

Affirmations are simple yet powerful statements that are designed to replace negative beliefs with empowering ones. When repeated consistently, they penetrate the subconscious mind, reprogramming it for positivity.

You will want to build your own affirmative statements but to get you started here are some top tips I use.

- I use the Present Tense. Phrase your affirmations as if the desired outcome is already true (e.g., "I am confident and capable").
- Be Specific and Positive. I focus on what I want, not what I don't want (e.g., "I am allowed to be successful" rather than "I don't want to fail").
- Feel the Emotion. I visualize and feel the truth of the affirmation as I say it. This strengthens its impact on the subconscious.

This is how I incorporate affirmations into my daily routine:

- I say them aloud (I sometimes shout them!) in front of a mirror each morning. Don't be shy about this. It's like singing in the shower, only you (and your subconscious mind) are listening
- I have them written down in my journal (more on that later) and on sticky notes placed around my home - like the fridge door.
- I repeat them during moments of self-doubt or before challenging situations.

Over time, you will find that affirmations can reshape your inner dialogue, boost self-confidence, and foster a more optimistic mindset and a more assertive attitude.

3. Visualization

Visualization is the practice of mentally rehearsing positive outcomes or experiences. It works because the subconscious mind responds to vivid imagery as if it were real, creating new neural pathways that support your goals. I find the perfect time to visualize is after my morning meditation session. My mind has been cleared of junk and I'm ready to move on. I will visualize what I want to achieve during the day to come. "I need to meet that deadline, I need to complete that report, I must pick up the Grandkids from school or whatever".

For bigger picture stuff I find the evening wind down after lights out is the time to visualize the desired outcomes.

These are the steps I follow for effective visualization:

- I set a clear goal. I decide what I want to visualize, whether it's achieving a professional milestone - another book, improving and maintaining health, feeling confident in social situations or feeling more assertive in a confrontational situation.
- I engage all senses. I imagine not just what the goal looks like but also how it feels, sounds, and even smells.
- I try to practice at least once a day. Just try 5–10 minutes each day to visualize your desired outcome. The more detailed and consistent your practice, the stronger the impact.

Remember this

- Sportsmen & women use visualization to enhance performance by mentally rehearsing successful outcomes. It clearly helps them and you can see them visualizing at the start line or before they serve or take the shot. I can share a personal experience here. I play golf and love the game. Many years ago, just after taking up the game, I regularly played a local 9 hole course. The third hole was a par 3. There was a large stream, about 10 feet wide running across the fairway about 75 yards from the Tee. I'm not a long hitter so for me it's a 5 or 7 Iron to the Green. This was my bogey hole. No matter how hard, soft, left or right I hit the ball I ended up in the stream. This went on for weeks with my subconscious mind at the helm making sure I went in the water. Playing Partners would wager by tossing a coin would I be in or out of the stream. Whoever called "IN" won the bet! That was until a fellow player took pity on me and advised me to visualize the shot - It worked!

- Professionals use it to build confidence before presentations or interviews. It's a practice I use. Before a presentation I will take a few minutes to breathe. I inhale for the count of 5, hold for the count of 5 and exhale for the count of 7 to 9 to squeeze all the air from my lungs. I do this 5 times and then visualize a successful presentation. It works for me, you should try it some time.

3

Chapter 3: Reprogramming the Subconscious

1. Hypnosis and Self-Hypnosis

Let me say upfront that I wondered long and hard whether or not to include this section in my book. On balance, I have decided to reference the topic as I believe some readers may find this a valuable resource on their own journey to well-being.

On my personal journey to a state of enhanced well-being I have become aware of hypnosis and have been hypnotized by a trained and qualified therapist. Hypnosis, as described to me by the therapist, "is a state of deep relaxation that bypasses the critical conscious mind, allowing direct access to the subconscious. In this state, the mind is more receptive to suggestions that promote positive change". It is most certainly not a stage act that makes people behave like a duck or a mad cow or whatever. Clearly, these stage performances can be entertaining and baffling both at the same time but I see no room for them in this arena.

In my experience of hypnosis I sensed a deep sense of relaxation and calm but no more so than I can achieve through meditation which some may see as a form of self hypnosis. I was given the information below that some readers may find helpful.

Steps for Self-Hypnosis:

- Create a Relaxing Environment: Find a quiet space where you won't be interrupted.
- Use a Script or Recording: Listen to a guided hypnosis track or repeat affirmations in a calm, steady voice.
- Visualize Your Desired Outcome: Allow your mind to imagine achieving your goal with clarity and emotion.

I will just finish this section by saying that, overall, It was a very pleasurable experience. It certainly didn't hurt but it did cost in both time and money!

2. Free Writing, Journaling and Mind Mapping

I wrote this book using some of the techniques described in this short chapter. If you have never "Free Written" I urge you to try it. It is an amazing process that reveals all sorts of hidden gems. Free writing allows your mind to spill onto the page without filters or constraints. Journaling is a powerful way to harness free writing to uncover subconscious patterns and bring clarity to your thoughts and emotions.

This is how I started and continue my journaling for aiding my journey to, and maintenance of, a state of well-being.

- I set a prompt using questions like "What's holding me back?" or "What do I need to let go of?" or "What do I want to achieve in a given circumstance?"
- I Free Write by hand. I feel it is much more personal if I use pen and paper. Actually I use A5 size bound notebooks with a pen strap. If I have something to write, I don't want to spend time

looking for a pen. I carry the journal with me when traveling and at home it is prominently sitting on my desk in the study. I don't worry about grammar, structure, or making sense - I just let my thoughts flow. Once captured I can correct the stuff to make it a sensible entry into my journal. That in itself can be an invigorating process watching the often incoherent become coherent. The word is definitely mightier than the sword.

- Having corrected and made sense of my Free Writing I read over the content to identify recurring themes or beliefs.
- I periodically glance back to previous entries (sometimes from years back) to see how things panned out and to remind me of some of the milestones I have passed on my journey to well-being.

I find that Journaling helps illuminate subconscious fears, desires, and motivations,which have given me a clearer picture of what needs to shift for greater well-being.

Mind Mapping is also a very powerful tool. It's how I structured this book. I find it an invaluable process for use in my work and play. I use it to define projects, outline PowerPoint presentations, create public speeches, plan events, record discussions, and make notes. If you have never Mind Mapped then you have never lived! I began Mind Mapping in the 1990s and have never looked back. The concept is based on and reflects how the brain works and it works! Read Tony Buzan - he developed the process, you won't regret it.

4

Chapter 4: Cultivating well-being Through Subconscious Alignment

Remember, at the beginning of the book, I gave the Oxford Dictionary definition of well-being and said that I thought it was much more than that. In this chapter I want to expand on those thoughts.

Greater minds than mine have put their shoulder to the wheel. Way back in history, the philosopher Aristotle came up with the concept of Eudaimonia - the contented state of feeling healthy, happy and prosperous. Others, such as Maslow, expanded on this concept by suggesting that although happiness is an integral part of your personal well-being, it includes other things such as the fulfillment of long-term goals, your sense of purpose and how in control you feel in life.

These pillars of wisdom can be morphed into a number of dimensions that reflect the deeper complexities that great thinkers had in mind.

Physical. This includes lifestyle choices that affect the functioning of our bodies. Smoking, drinking and substance usage together with what we eat, how we sleep and how active we are will affect our physical well-being.

I want to add a note here specifically about sleep. I can't stress enough the importance of quality sleep. I used to suffer from insomnia as a young man. It came from nowhere and about 18 months later it just went. No idea what caused it or why. I believe quality sleep is essential for the proper functioning of the subconscious mind. During sleep, the brain is still actively processing and consolidating experiences, memories, reinforcing learning and emotional regulation. I have found that a consistent evening routine is more important than quantity. I usually get up within minutes of waking up and say (even shout) out loud "Today is going to be a Great Day" as I pump both fists into the air. It puts a smile on my face which is a good start to any day!

Emotional. This is our ability to cope with everyday life and reflects how we think and feel about ourselves.

Social. This is the extent that we feel a sense of purpose, belonging, recognition and social inclusion. The way we communicate with others, our relationships, values, beliefs, lifestyles and traditions are all important factors of social well-being. In my view, you might consider ditching social media. Better to have a few real friends that you meet or speak to regularly rather than an army of followers and strangers! By all means use technology to maintain those friendships but do not be seduced into the sewer that social media has become.

Spiritual. I'm referring to the "spark within" covering the ability to experience and integrate meaning and sense of purpose in life. This is achieved through being connected to our inner self, to nature and, for some, an even greater power.

Intellectual. Every day is a school day! It is important to gain and maintain intellectual well-being as it helps us to expand our knowledge and skills in order to live an enjoyable and successful life. Study or practice something everyday.

Economic. Economic well-being, in short, is our ability to meet our basic needs and feel a sense of security. How that is achieved will vary from person to person. For most our primary resource will be our job (for some it will be "just over broke"). Easily said but I would urge you to seek employment that gives you a sense of satisfaction/well-being, whatever that employment may be. Depending on your age this section may be critical. My Grandchildren (five & three years old) will be part of a generation that can expect living to 100 and beyond as the norm. That's assuming we haven't either fried planet earth or blown it to pieces before then. Gone are the days of a "job for life". Workers can expect to work to 80 before retirement and with the advent of AI and Automation expect to have several careers backed by continuous training in new skills. Or there is a paradigm shift with people working two days a week and having five days off along with 12 weeks vacation. Who knows what the future holds; consider this last part as food for thought.

So how can we bind this all together? I have detailed below a number of strategies that I suggest you begin to implement and begin with yourself.

1. Self-Compassion and Gratitude

Be kind to yourself (and others). I have found that a compassionate inner voice nurtures emotional resilience and self-acceptance. In other words you are what you are but you can be what you can be! When you treat yourself with kindness, your subconscious begins to internalize messages of worthiness and love and as a result strengthens and affirms our ability to move forward under adversity.

I practice a little self-compassion by:

- Occasionally writing a letter to myself as if I were a supportive friend. Pointing out what is going well, how I have overcome similar events in the past. I have found this particularly helpful during times of stress or after mistakes have been made.
- Acknowledging those mistakes and forgiving myself by affirming

my intention to learn.
- Using my Journal to record all.
- And I remember that old cliche "What doesn't kill you makes you stronger"

I find that being grateful is another powerful tool for enhancing well-being. I regularly focus on what I'm grateful for. It encourages my subconscious to notice positivity in my life. When feeling down or hard done by I always take the view that if I were to turn around 360 degrees I would see someone who was worse off than me.

So try this:

- Keep a gratitude note in your journal where you list three things you're thankful for each day. Might be the same three things every day but simply by repeating them you reinforce them.
- Take notice. Remember the simple things that give you joy. Might be those leaves you saw earlier floating down a stream. Reflect on those moments, big or small, before sleep.

2. Building Resilience Through Forgiveness

Just as I have urged you to be kind and forgive yourself, you need to be able to forgive others. To be clear, I'm not suggesting you forgive the guy who, for example, murdered your brother. My brother was killed while taking his dog for a walk. (The best I can hope for here is that I forget the guy and just remember my brother; and this is another perfect example of the power of the subconscious mind. It holds all our memories - good and bad. It has the ability to mask the bad memories from our day to day lives so that we can continue with our day to day living and not be crippled by bad memories). I'm talking about the person who may have slighted you in some way, pushed in front of you, or suffered Road Rage from. Forgiveness is a gift you have available to give yourself and to others. Holding onto resentment or guilt weighs down the subconscious, creating barriers to happiness and well-being.

I find it easy to practice forgiveness:

- By meditating on the person or situation I need to forgive and imagining what it feels like to release the burden.
- I affirm my intention to let go and move forward, such as "I free myself from the pain of the past."

Letting go frees up mental and emotional energy, creating space for growth and joy.

3. By Growing As a Person.

Consider the following strategies that I practice. You will grow to be more rounded, tolerant, compassionate and empathetic and your well-being will be enhanced as a result.

Establish Links. Acknowledge passers by with a greeting or just a smile and a nod. Talk and listen to others. Remember why you have two ears and only one mouth! Always live in the moment.

Keep Learning. As mentioned earlier, every day is a school day. Since starting my journey I have taken up painting and playing the bass guitar (badly I might add) learning Bulgarian - I have reached the reading age of a five year old in Bulgarian!

Get Active. Please, please, please do something! Walk, run, cycle, lift weights, swim, stretch, Pilates, Yoga, Golf, Tennis, anything that gets you off your butt and outdoors (preferably) and do it regularly. I have found that getting up early, stretching, and going for a 20 minute brisk walk before breakfast sets me up for the day. I do this six days a week regardless of the weather. Getting a good soaking can be quite cathartic.

Give. Give your time, your words and your presence to people. Consider giving to worthy causes, and volunteer to help others. In simple terms - do the right thing!

5

Chapter 5: Real-Life Benefits of Subconscious Work

So this is what I have found since I started my journey to the state of well-being:

Improved Relationships. By reprogramming beliefs about worthiness and trust I have transformed how I connect with others. I approach relationships with more confidence, authenticity, and empathy.

By utilizing visualization and positive thinking I have reduced stress, lowered my blood pressure, and improved overall health by engaging the mind-body connection.

Goal Achievement. By aligning my subconscious with my goals I have ensured that my actions are rooted in belief and clarity, propelling me toward success.

6

Chapter 6: Overcoming Doubt and Building Trust in the Process

Addressing Doubt

"Ah yes but…..". I can hear you now! Doubt is a natural reaction when trying something new. To overcome it I suggest you do the following:

- Start with small, achievable goals to build confidence.
- Celebrate incremental progress, no matter how minor.
- Surround yourself with positive influences, such as books, podcasts, or mentors who inspire growth.

Dealing with Cynicism

Cynicism often stems from past disappointments or fear of failure. To address it:

- Keep an open mind. Remind yourself that change takes time.
- Document your journey. Reflect on subtle shifts, like improved moods or reduced stress.
- Commit to consistency. Results come through daily practice.

7

Conclusion

Conclusion
So there it is - my journey to enhanced well-being through the medium of "Your Hidden Mind". Your journey, should you undertake it, requires patience, trust, and an open heart—but the rewards are transformative. The subconscious mind is a powerful ally in your journey toward well-being. By understanding its influence, cultivating self-awareness, and employing practices like meditation, affirmations, and visualization, you can unlock its potential for positive change. Every step you take brings you closer to a life filled with joy, health, and purpose. The journey begins now

I won't wish you good luck, I will wish you a successful journey.

If you found this guide helpful I would be grateful if you could leave a positive review on Amazon in order to help other people.

Resources:
   Professor Hans Eyesenk (Being Human)
   https://www.everand.com *Why being smart is not an accident and how*

to use your brain correctly for peak success. (n.d.). Everand. https://wellbeingpeople.com*THE MEANING OF WELLBEING IS MULTIDIMENSIONAL.* (n.d.). Wellbeing People. Retrieved December 2, 2024, from https://wellbeingpeople.com

www.ingramcontent.com/pod-product-compliance
Lightning Source LLC
Chambersburg PA
CBHW072345270726
48659CB00023B/2396